Zoom for Beginners

2020/2021

A Step-By-Step Guide to Easily Start Virtual Meetings with Zoom. Learn How to Plan and Manage Video Webinars, Conferences, and Live Streams

Beverly Brown

Table of Contents

Introduction

"If you are in a position where you can reach people, then use your platform to stand up for a cause." - Germany Kent

Kent spoke truly, but remember that causes aren't always extravagant social movements. All businesses are built to fulfill a need, and the desire to meet this need becomes a cause in its own right.

As technology marches on, and as workplace conditions shift throughout the globe, video conferencing is becoming an increasingly useful tool for trained professionals and students alike in making connections and gaining support for both personal and common goals. Video conferencing cuts down dramatically on the jet-fuel prices typically associated with international business meetings, and even on the local level it allows you to streamline reports from your colleagues in an efficient yet personal manner.

Without video conferencing, it'd be harder to maintain that ineffably important aspect of "human touch" among those working from home or using flexi-hours. Meetings would remain inefficient due to factors such as transport, weather or traffic jams. And students who are ill or need to remain home due to extenuating circumstances wouldn't be able to touch base with their teachers so that they remain aware of where they stand in terms of coursework.

With video-conferencing, however, you can enjoy the ability to keep contact with audiences, assets, human resources and more, without geography negatively impacting their usefulness. When used properly, video conferencing simplifies the management and coordination process, taking a great deal of stress off your shoulders by reassuring you that everyone is on the same page, and that there is no ambiguity in the tasks that need doing. After all, a two-way call between you and your group allows your instructions to be contextualized through voice, tone and facial expression, while any questions they may have can be resolved simply through letting them ask. Contrast to emails or message systems, which are notorious for becoming addictive, disrupting workflow and impairing concentration.

So, if video conferencing is so potent, why haven't you begun using such a powerful tool yet? The truth is, not everyone is comfortable with new technology, especially if it requires having to discard old knowledge and relearn how to do things. Perhaps you already use some form of telecommunication or social media to try to get your message across to others, yet haven't found much success in using such technology to unite your colleagues, your classes or your workforce. Or maybe it is successful, but your current method is inefficient, and you're looking for insight on something better. Perhaps you have used similar, fairly efficient tech in the past, but were never sure how it worked, and thus do not feel confident you'd use Zoom meetings optimally on your own, right off the bat. Maybe you're afraid of getting off on the wrong foot, or creating the wrong impression due to "technical difficulties."

Fear not! This book is designed to teach you all you need to know to set up, host, and record your very own video conference, and so much more! By the time you finish the final chapter, you'll have all the knowledge necessary to handle virtual communication with ease, all through the ubiquitous and incredibly versatile Zoom software.

Zoom is a simple program that is fun and intuitive to use, yet it holds such a wide array of features that many may slip beneath your notice. This book aims to explain the vast majority of these features to you as they are, at the time writing, from the perspective of a current and active user. If Zoom's user manuals feel too daunting, too technical or too impersonal, here you will find simple, easy-to-understand step-by-step guides that'll walk you through everything you'll need to know. Before explaining how to install and use the software, however, let us first go over why you should use Zoom software and services.

It is recommended that you begin working with Zoom as soon as possible; we live in an ever-innovative world, where technology is constantly changing and adapting. The sooner you learn this knowledge, the better the foundation you can lay for yourself with the information within.

Chapter 1: What is Zoom?

Zoom, Explained

Zoom Video Communications, or "Zoom" for short, is a cloud-based communications service that was founded by a man named Eric Yuan in 2011. According to Eric, this decision was influenced during his late teen years by his girlfriend, who he only got to see twice a year, and even then would need to endure a ten-hour train ride just to see her face. Although he would go through all this for her, Eric could not stop thinking, "Wouldn't it have been nice if I could've just touched a button, and suddenly, I could see her? Talk to her?"

Coming from such a warm and personal place in its CEO's heart, it should be no surprise that Zoom's stated mission and vision is to create, maintain and develop services that will revolutionize real-time, face-to-face collaboration and communication. Zoom intends to improve both the quality and the potency of our verbal correspondence for the foreseeable future so that people across the globe are better able to share information, come together and achieve greater deeds.

When asked about their values, the company has responded, "We care for our company, our customers, our community, our teammates and ourselves" (Zoom Video Communications, 2020).

Advantages, Disadvantages

Now, that is all well and good, but how does it translate into Zoom's quality as a product? Quite well, it turns out.

Even compared to conferencing apps such as Google Hangouts, Zoom boasts stronger, clearer audio and a higher, smoother visual quality. As if that wasn't quite enough, Zoom also manages to beat Hangouts in terms of sheer amount of call participants. Zoom allows you to enable a video call with up to a hundred individuals at once, which is perfect for large classes, assemblies, religious gatherings, large extended family reunions and department/division meetings. Out of those 100, you can elect to see the faces of 49 at your will, making it easy to see the mental space everyone is in. Hangouts, in contrast, will only allow twenty-five people on a call at once.

Zoom will even win in terms of advanced features (many of which we'll be covering a little later), such as a built-in annotator so that you can take notes spontaneously without need for pen, paper or even an open Word Document, which can be a powerful boon depending on your participants' available resources. For the host, Zoom also offers the ability to create full transcripts of meetings for easy rollback, revision or review. Like Hangouts, Zoom also offers cloud storage and recording for paid subscribers, which it enables automatically, when applicable.

In situations where you need to see each other's workstations rather than each other's faces, Zoom once again wins by allowing multiple users to share screens at once, something which Hangouts simply cannot do. This feature makes virtual exhibits possible and streamlines virtual presentations as each presenter can ready their content beforehand, cutting back on the time wasted setting up and tearing down slideshows and the like.

The story is similar when compared to an app like Discord, which again only allows twenty-five people into a call at once, and has the added downside of mostly being a gaming hub, meaning the temptation for a co-worker to get distracted during a call will be higher. Now, of course, this will always be an issue to some degree with videoconferencing, but it's noted as especially disadvantageous here because here the temptation is built-in to the service, rather than instead remaining within a third-party app that colleagues are generally more likely to ignore.

Zoom is best for that professional, focused tone, and the ability to replace your background with a virtual one of your choosing, can aid you in setting the stage and creating the correct mood. This concept of focus is reinforced by the fact that, by default, Zoom will only let you have one meeting active at a time, and does not have any chat feature that isn't directly tied into a specific meeting. This is a huge advantage over services like Skype, Facebook Messenger or WhatsApp, all of which have that addictive factor that comes with free and unfiltered instant messaging (and yes, Discord suffers from this, too).

Do not fret however; if you belong to a support corps of some kind, or act as general moderating/support staff, there is a way to enable joining multiple meetings at once, for when you need to be able to observe multiple gatherings in real-time. Even then, you are less likely to get distracted or lose focus compared to other apps, as again you'll still be operating in the confines of professional meetings.

But how does Zoom compare to Skype when held up against one another completely? After all, they are the closest in terms of intended use and overall goal. Both have crisp user interfaces, and both make video calls a dream. One advantage Skype has over Zoom is in its instant messaging, however that is also a double-edged sword as described earlier; especially if users do not keep a Skype profile for business separate from a profile for personal use. That said, Skype is one of the few platforms to allow more participants than Zoom (up to 250), but only if you subscribe to its paid version. Zoom, as mentioned, allows a hundred participants in your meeting for free, and allows 500 or more with add-on packs if you're running Pro or higher.

Zoom, overall, is the absolute ace for video conferences. Not only due to its consistently higher attendance capacity, but also due to the sheer amount of control and customization you gain over how your meetings are hosted. If you ever thought managing a hundred participants sounds tough, do not fret; Zoom allows you to mute and unmute participants at your will, as well as grant every participant the ability to raise a virtual hand when they wish to add input into the meeting, meaning the environment can operate much as it does in a real meeting hall or classroom where everyone can use signs and symbols to communicate a desire to speak, without disrupting the proceedings or throwing off the current speaker.

Zoom's Biggest Advantage

Zoom's biggest advantage, however, is that participants do not need to have a registered account with it in order to take part in your meetings. With other platforms, you'll occasionally have that one person who doesn't have Skype, or doesn't use Discord. In these cases, registry can be a hassle that can reduce interest or even cause delays. Zoom bypasses this by letting anyone show up to a meeting, as long as they know the meeting ID. At your discretion, you can even rule for a meeting to be accessible via browser, meaning the Zoom app wouldn't even need to be downloaded by your participants at all, which is a great boost in convenience for them, and therefore more faces and fewer headaches for you. "I don't have/couldn't install the communication app" will never again be a cause for absence or delay.

If such convenient access sounds risky, do not worry; there are very easy and unobtrusive security measures you can implement to ensure only your intended participants can fully join, and the process for enabling these measures will be described in later chapters.

What You Can Expect From Zoom's Free Model

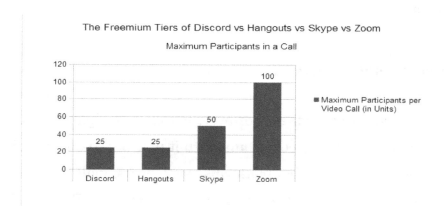

The Freemium Tiers of Discord vs Hangouts vs Skype vs Zoom

Maximum Participants in a Call

If you still feel unsure about Zoom, here are the features you can expect to enjoy while testing out its free model; to start off, although you can only host one meeting at a time, and although each meeting will only last for 40 minutes, there is no limit to the number of meetings you can host in total over time. This means you can theoretically use Zoom's free version forever, if you so desire. The 40-minute limit is also waived for meetings with three participants or fewer, allowing an infinite conversation when the group is tiny and intimate.

You can save recordings and transcripts for your meetings locally, meaning they'll be stored on your computer or device, and you can share those recordings and transcripts with others via email later at no cost.

You can expect visual and aural quality in HD, at 720p for the former, and Zoom will seamlessly detect and enlarge the portrait of whoever is currently speaking, bringing them to the foreground and ensuring they hold the attention of the floor. All other features pertaining to Zoom mentioned before this point are also included in the free package.

For security, you get to add a waiting room for eager participants, so that you can cross-check them and ensure they aren't uninvited guests; the meetings themselves are protected by SSL and AES encryption.

You can also create group chats, which behave similarly to instant messaging apps, except they're usually centered around the kind of meetings you hold, keeping the professional tone as well as encouraging a degree of separation from social media during work hours.

If this sounds good to you, note that the Zoom application is available for almost every device, as it works on Windows, Linux, Macs, Android and iOS devices.

Is Free Enough for Me?

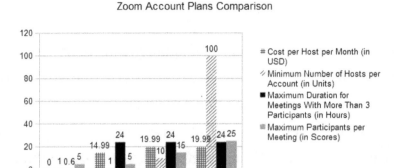

For the vast majority of users, the free version of Zoom is sufficient. Even if you plan on hosting a meeting of more than three people for longer than forty minutes, a great and comfortable way to work around the free version of Zoom's time limit is to allow a short 5-15 minute break after your first forty minutes expire, and then simply start a new meeting on the same topic thereafter, as you'll find that there's nothing preventing you from doing so.

Teachers, students and entrepreneurs in their early stages can likely get by happily on the free version of Zoom with little trouble.

However, there are another three tiers to be aware of, just in case they'd be better for your specific situation; **Pro**, **Business** and **Enterprise**. Pricing plans can be found on Zoom's pricing page.

Pro is sufficient for groups and organizations that have a fairly small number of leaders or managers; for instance, a high school might only have nine teachers assigned to its senior grades, and a local business might have a similarly-sized managerial staff. In addition to having all the free version's features, Pro also allows meetings to run up to 24 hours at a time; far longer than most would ever consider holding a meeting outside of Congress. Additionally, you, as a host, are provided 1 GB of storage on Zoom's cloud, making it easier to record and distribute your meetings after they end (as if that wasn't easy enough before). You also have the option to host up to 1,000 participants and gain greater cloud storage space if you're willing to pay a little extra for add-ons. Finally, this is the tier where Zoom's Webinar feature becomes available, and you begin gaining specialized admin tools that let you delegate limited host powers to select non-host participants.

This makes Pro an excellent choice over the free version if you need to reinforce a more serious atmosphere, have longer talks with large groups of associates without interruptions, or otherwise wish to ensure conferences remain orderly through empowered delegation of responsibility.

Business, meanwhile, has all the free and Pro features, gives you dedicated customer support (meaning response will be faster and more sensitive to your issues), as well as the ability to weave the brand of your company into the meeting, such as with custom URLs, meeting pages and invitation formats. It requires ten hosts at a minimum however, each of which will need to pay the monthly subscription, meaning this option is best for large, wealthy organizations who have already established themselves in their field. This is a great option for larger organizations who need a competitive edge, more complex administrative hierarchies during meetings, or a stronger professional image during said meetings through branding.

The **Enterprise** tier, however, should only be considered by extremely large multinational corporations with strong international interest and investment due to its high cost and host requirements. Enterprise's biggest advantage over Business is the sheer size of participants it can host (although similar amounts can be hosted cheaper on lower tiers through add-ons), as well as limitless cloud storage and discounts on Webinar and Zoom Room add-ons, which could end up saving money for exceptionally large businesses, if they rely on hosting seminars for hundreds or even thousands of people at a time; although for most organizations this won't be the case.

Chapter 2: Getting Started

Installing Zoom

For some, downloading a new app can be scary, but do not fret. Installing Zoom is an exceptionally simple process, and this subheading is just to assure you that you're on the right track. Remember, installing Zoom is only necessary if you need to host a meeting, or if whoever is hosting the meeting you wish to attend doesn't allow you to join via browsers like Google.

To install Zoom, start by opening your browser. You can then navigate your way to this link: https://zoom.us/download. From here, click on "Zoom Client for Meetings" if you are using Windows, Linux or Mac. If you're using Android or iOS, you can instead download "Zoom Mobile Apps," although you can also do this from your Android App Store or Google Play.

Your application will naturally begin downloading, and comes to around 13 MB in size. For Windows, Linux and Mac users, you'll notice that the downloaded file is an .exe called "ZoomInstaller.exe." When it has finished downloading, double-click on it so that it can run the Zoom installation process on your computer.

From this point, you're almost ready to use Zoom. If you want to host meetings or unlock other functions beyond being a participant, you'll need to register for a Zoom account. If your newly-installed Zoom App doesn't give you a prompt to do so, you can register at this link: https://zoom.us/signup. Fill in the data truthfully. You will then be given the opportunity to sign up using either your professional email address, a Google account or a Facebook account. If you have permission to use your company's domain or email address, you can also sign up via SSO. Choose one of these methods according to your needs and abilities, and follow the prompts and instructions, answering questions truthfully (e.g. "Are you signing up on behalf of a school?").

You'll be sent an email asking for verification. Log onto the relevant email account, open the email from *no-reply@zoom.us* and click "Activate Account." From there, a browser tab will open asking you to fill in your desired first and last name, as well as a password. If you're using Google Chrome, a secure password will automatically be generated for you, and you won't need to remember it. Continue, and you'll now have full access to Zoom's free tier. You'll also receive an optional prompt to invite several of your colleagues to Zoom, which is a great idea if you want to get your workmates collaborating on Zoom faster, but can otherwise be skipped.

Hosting Your Very First Conference

Now that you have signed up for a Zoom account, Zoom will ask you if you wish to start your test meeting. In your web browser, you'll be provided with a meeting URL as well as an option to launch your meeting (namely, an orange button named "Start Meeting Now"). Select it, and allow the browser tab that opens to start your Zoom application. You should then sign in automatically, but if not simply double-click the "Sign In" button. In your newly-installed Zoom app, you'll soon see a crisp white page with a host of details such as Meeting Password, your Participant ID, Host Name and more. You'll also see options to invite participants, share screens or join audio. As you're the only person in your meeting, and thus it has not truly begun yet, you'll find that even though you're using the free version of Zoom, the meeting timer is not counting down, so be sure to take your time as you familiarize yourself with your app's dashboard.

At this stage, you may wish to ensure that your audio is working properly, and that your webcam is working, if you want people to be able to see your face. To ensure your audio is fine, mouse over to the Mute button, which will appear in the bottom left corner of your Zoom app by default. On the Mute icon, you'll see a little arrow (like this ^) to the right of the microphone symbol. Click on that arrow. A box will then open, showing you the enabled microphones and speakers your device is connected to. Usually, Zoom will have already selected, or ticked the correct speaker and microphone for you to use, but if not, you now have the power to change it. To ensure that your audio is meeting-ready, click on "Test Speaker & Microphone," which is still located in this same little box. Zoom will then play a sound. If you cannot hear it, make sure that your speakers are plugged in properly, are undamaged, have up-to-date drivers and have been selected under "Select a Speaker," which you'd have seen when you first clicked on that little arrow in the Mute icon. Zoom, for its part, will cycle through your various speaker options if you click "No."

Once you have sound, click "Yes." A similar process will play out with your microphone; simply follow the instructions, and keep the troubleshooting methods mentioned above in mind. Before clicking "Yes" however, have your computer make a few sounds (e.g. play a YouTube video for a few seconds). If your microphone picks that up and plays it back to you, then consider either moving your speakers further away or investing in earbuds or headphones so that your microphone only captures your voice, and not your speakers. Otherwise, a nasty audial feedback loop will be created whenever people speak in the meeting, causing much pain for everyone.

Finally, in this same small dark box you set your Speakers/Microphone in, select "Audio Settings." From here, you can perform finer tweaks on speaker and microphone volume, just for Zoom. You'll also see other kinds of settings, such as Recording or Video. Under Recording, choose where all recorded files from Zoom will be stored on your device, and choose whether you want a separate recording for each participant's voice or not. You're now nearly ready to host a meeting, but something is missing; your beautiful face. If you cannot see your face in Zoom Meetings, check next to the Mute icon. To its right, you'll see a Start/Stop Video icon. Make sure you have a webcam either integrated into your device (e.g. most mobile devices and many laptops), or you have a webcam connected with the correct drivers installed (which you'll need to do for most desktops).

Then, go back into Video Settings, and tweak them to your liking. You are now fully ready for your first meeting. Note that you can turn off your webcam or microphone via Zoom whenever you wish through clicking on either the Stop/Start Video or Mute icon respectively, and that Audio and Video settings have options to ensure your microphone or webcam is disabled when you first start up each meeting, if you so choose.

Whenever you wish to host a meeting from this point, simply Sign In on your Zoom App. If you had Google Chrome auto-generate your account password, you can find it saved under Autofill if you type *chrome://settings* into your browser's URL bar. Once signed in to Zoom, just click on New Meeting.

You'll notice that the friendly Invite icon that your test meeting provided you might no longer appear, but do not panic. To invite participants, click on "Participants," which you'll see on your meeting taskbar between "Security" and "Chat." This will bring up a white tab on the right of your meeting room. At the bottom left of this white tab is a small, unobtrusive "Invite" button. Click on it, and you'll see a Contacts list. This will likely be empty for you at first, so instead either click on the Email tab, which is just to the right of Contacts, or click on either *Copy Invite Link* or *Copy Invitation*. Email is best if you intend to invite people by, well, email, while Copy Invitation is best if you want to invite people to your meeting via a third-party Instant Messaging app. You can paste your invitation wherever you like, even in a Word document, and from there you can see what information you'll need to share with prospective participants.

Copy Invite Link is similar in function to Copy Invitation; but as the name implies, it only provides the link, whereas the Invitation additionally gives information such as Meeting ID or Passcode, which can be useful depending on how your audience likes to connect.

The link is generally enough for most users, as it'll directly bring them into either your Meeting or its Waiting Room if enabled, so long as they have a browser as they'll need to plug the link into their browser's URL bar. A Meeting ID, however, lets one join a meeting using their Zoom App directly by selecting either "Sign In" or "Join a Meeting," joining a meeting and then pasting the ID in the bar that asks for it. Note that when Zoom explicitly asks for a Meeting ID, providing a URL or link instead may cause shenanigans, such as asking for a password when you have not set or enabled one. IDs are therefore best sent to people who already have Zoom and know how it works, while links work best for first-time or inexperienced participants. However, links remove the requirement for users to know a password, meaning security is more tenuous if the link or URL gets leaked. Meeting IDs, in contrast, require passcodes by default before users will be admitted.

Scheduling & Connecting

Invite Links, despite potential security risks, are especially useful among universally trustworthy or tight-knit groups as they simplify the joining process for participants. Note that the link will prompt them to download and install Zoom, although once again they do not need to register to join your meeting. If for whatever reason they cannot download Zoom, then below the prompt to download in their browser, your prospective participant will see (in small print), "If you cannot download or run the application, join from your browser." If they don't see this option immediately, it should appear when they try to click on "launch Zoom" in that same browser page.

They must then click the underlined part of the quote above (in their browser), and they'll be able to join without having to download anything at all. This is a true boon for those who wish to stay accessible and convenient, and if you are a teacher it'll certainly make the lives of your students easier, especially those who live in areas with sub-par internet and therefore may struggle with downloads.

If your work or position requires regular meetings, as opposed to ad hoc ones, you can schedule them quite easily by signing in to your Zoom app and then clicking on "Schedule." You can then set the date, time and duration of your meeting, although beware that you have selected the appropriate time zone too so that there are no misunderstandings. If you know and trust your participants, and meet with them regularly, feel free to use your Personal Meeting ID. Otherwise, opt to have your meeting's ID be automatically generated instead. Your Personal Meeting ID lets people join into your private, constant meeting room - at any time the meeting is active, no less - so you do not wish to expose that to strangers. An automatically generated ID, however, does not carry that kind of risk, as auto-generated IDs update and change, trading some convenience for more security.

Once your video, audio and password settings for this meeting are as you desire, for further security it is recommended you click on "Advanced Options" and enable the Waiting Room, and ensure Join Before Host remains disabled. It's also recommended that you keep the password requirement enabled, and set it to whatever you wish.

From there, decide which calendar you wish to add your scheduled meeting to, noting that anyone with a Google Account automatically has Google Calendar too. Once scheduled in your calendar, you can then either notify participants by adding their email addresses in the calendar slot that asks for guests/invitees, or you can share the invite information with others normally via an instant messaging program. Ensure that the information you share with your future participants includes the meeting's password, if you kept that option enabled.

Connecting to a scheduled meeting, from the user's end, is much like connecting to a non-scheduled or Instant meeting; they can do so either via invite link or via ID, with the caveat that they cannot join before the schedule says the meeting will start.

Connecting - Your Home Page

You'll notice that, in addition to creating, joining or scheduling meetings, you also have the option to Share Screens. This allows people to see your computer screen the same way you do. You can also choose whether or not people can hear your computer as you do when you screen share by clicking on the little downwards arrow next to the "Share Screen" option and checking "Share computer sounds," which is enabled by default. The little arrow next to "New meeting" will also let you change your mind on decisions such as whether or not to use your Personal Meeting ID during instant meetings, as well as whether or not to start with your webcam disabled. If you hover your mouse over the 10-11 digit number below that, however, you'll also find quick and easy ways to copy Meeting ID and invitation, as well as give you an option to tweak your Personal Meeting space under PMI settings.

Connecting - Beginner Tips for Students and Teachers

When holding a class, here are some general tips to follow: first, it's recommended that all participants are automatically muted when initially entering the meeting. If you did not set participants to automatically be muted upon entry when scheduling your meeting (which you can do under Advanced Options when scheduling), you can instead click on the Participants icon in the taskbar at the bottom of the meeting screen. Right next to where you saw Invite last time, you'll see the option to Mute All. Next to Mute All is a small ellipse that will show you further options as a host. Here you can see, again, the option to mute participants automatically as they come in.

Enabling this can save your students some embarrassment should they involuntarily cough/chortle/sneeze/fall over; when muted these things won't interrupt the lesson. If a student wishes to ask a question, they can either type it in the Meeting Chat and you, as a host, can keep an eye on the chat and answer questions that way, or for a more personal touch you can tell your students to virtually raise their hand. They can do this by clicking on Participants, and then navigating to the Raise Hand option, which they'll see at the bottom right of the window that pops up.

As a Host, you can then, in response to raised hands, intuitively mute and unmute participants by clicking next to their name and selecting the appropriate option.

When they are finished speaking, they can then navigate back and choose to Lower Hands so that the host knows it's alright to mute them again. If a participant using a mobile device wishes to Raise/Lower Hands, they can find the option to do so under the "More" button while the meeting is ongoing. See *Emotes* in Chapter 3 for a possible fix if this option isn't appearing for your participants.

Note that the option to Raise/Lower hands doesn't appear for the Host, just as how the option to Mute All under Participants doesn't appear to non-hosts.

Speaking of muting, while participants can unmute themselves, unless you disallow it under Mute All, they can never mute/unmute each other; they can only disable their entire personal audio if someone is bugging them, so a teacher can be sure to keep disruptive students in line so that more diligent ones don't feel driven away.

For students, remember that even if you may physically be at home, you are still effectively in class; by all means be yourself, but not at the expense of the class's learning process. Keep yourself muted when you do not have anything you want to share, and always think before you write in chat or speak out live; it is fully possible for Zoom Chat to be limited or disabled by the host if they feel it is being abused.

Chapter 3: Tips & Tricks

This chapter is written under the prerequisite that you are using your Zoom desktop app when you are the host. Features work similarly on mobile devices. It is not recommended for hosts to ever run their meetings through the browser, however, as they'll find their functionality is greatly limited. Running Zoom through your browser is only recommended if you are an attendee and are not expected to co-host.

Before we begin, note that most functions carry shortcuts that reduce the amount of clicking and navigation you have to do. To examine and set your shortcuts, open your Zoom App. Then, go to Settings, then to Keyboard Shortcuts. There, you'll see hotkey combinations that make your life easier once you remember them.

For instance, you can quickly mute or unmute yourself by pressing the Alt key and A simultaneously. Alt and Y Simultaneously will Raise/Lower your virtual hand. Alt+Shift+T, meanwhile, takes a screenshot. You can edit any of these hotkeys to anything you like. You can also choose whether these hotkeys are "enabled globally" or not.

What does that mean? Normally, most hotkey combinations won't work unless your Zoom app is your active tab (i.e. you clicked on it last). This prevents you from accidentally executing a Zoom command while typing somewhere else. When enabled globally, however, then the hotkey combination will always activate its respective command, even if you're currently busy in another app with Zoom in the background. Bear this in mind before you choose to edit any hotkeys/shortcuts.

As a general rule, any hotkey that you change to be a single button press (e.g. changing the mute/unmute action to just require pressing A, rather than Alt+A) should never be enabled globally, as it'd be inevitable that you'll eventually run the command by accident, possibly to detrimental effect. Now, onto the meat of this chapter.

Basic Security & Screen Sharing

Before we go onto how you, as a host, can deal with disruptive participants, it'd be prudent to first help you reduce the likelihood of unwanted guests showing up in the first place. A nasty phenomenon known as "Zoombombing" has been trending where a legitimate participant accidentally leaks your Meeting ID or URL to the wrong kind of person, and suddenly your meeting is full of people spamming the chat, filling up places intended for your colleagues or students, and posting obscene material through Zoom's file sharing service. Luckily, this nightmare of a scenario is very easy to prevent.

First, when possible, you should delay sharing your meeting password until about an hour or less before it is supposed to occur, and never share said password or even Meeting ID directly on public social media; rather get in touch with people privately via email or calendar, or share only within group chats that you trust. This reduces the chances of a leak.

Next, keeping passwords (a.k.a. passcodes) enabled means that even if people do know your Meeting ID, they still won't get in so easily; although, remember that meeting links automatically have your meeting passcode embedded in them.

The next thing you'll want, then, is to keep the Waiting Room feature enabled as this is a "safety zone" where you can view all interested participants and decide which ones get in or not. Sometimes a Zoombomber will try to sneak in using a familiar name, so if you feel unsure of a person's identity, either ask them to enable their camera or have them send you an Instant Message via other software to verify themselves.

Note that when the Waiting Room feature is enabled, it is impossible for participants to Join Before Host even if that latter option is also enabled, as only the host can let them pass through the waiting room. This is not only great for security, but also gives you a chance to perform last-minute tweaks to settings without looking unprofessional, as participants in the Waiting Room cannot see what you're doing in the meeting proper.

To ensure your Waiting Room is enabled for Instant meetings, go to Participants, navigate to the ellipses next to Mute All, then click on it. You'll remember this is how you accessed the Mute Participants Upon Entry option earlier. A bit below it, but in the same window, is the Enable Waiting Room option. If it doesn't have a tick next to it, click on it so it does. You can also Enable the Waiting Room during meetings by clicking on the Security icon, where you will see the option pop up.

Naturally, for Instant meetings it is best if you do not give out any meeting links or IDs until you are sure these features are in place.

For an extra layer of precaution, it is also recommended you navigate to Share Screen in the taskbar at the bottom of your meeting window, then click on the little arrow next to it. From there, make sure the "Who can share?" setting is set to "Only Host," and that only one participant may share at a time. You should set "Who can share?" to "All Participants" only in edge cases such as PowerPoint Presentations, although even then it is better if participants send their presentations to you as a host so that their presentation can be shown through your screen.

Do not allow All Participants to share screens as a general rule, as Zoombombers love exploiting this when they can to share pornography or graphically violent footage. When someone is sharing screens inappropriately, then you as a host can interrupt them by sharing your own screen; if you kept options set so that only one participant can share at a time, and if you left the default settings so that only the host can interrupt, then this'll mean opening your own screen will immediately shut down malicious screen-sharing attempts while you deal with the source. To share your screen, simply click on the green Share Screen option, then select the window you wish to share.

Outside of a security context, being able to select which window to share before sharing means you'll never accidentally show your messy desktop or reveal a sensitive document you accidentally left open; screen-sharing is contained to the window that the sharer specified.

Finally, once all intended participants are in your meeting, navigate back to the Enable Waiting Room option, whether through Participants or through Security. In the same window as the Waiting Room option is the "Lock Meeting" option. Enabling this will guarantee that no further individuals will be able to barge in, no matter what. This can be useful as, by default, both the host and participants alike have the power to Invite new attendees in (under the Participants tab) at any time. Sure, they'd just get caught by the Waiting Room anyway if enabled, but sometimes one can do without that kind of distraction.

Do not think twice about locking the meeting once all intended attendees are in. As a host, you can unlock the meeting at will, if necessary, ensuring that you're simply keeping trolls out, and not alienating intended participants who just happened to get unlucky with time management.

Admin Tools, Polls & Questionnaires

Dealing With Disruption

Sometimes, despite the precautions you take, you'll still have disruptive members in your meeting. You already know how to Mute, both selectively and unanimously, so you won't be bothered by the occasional good-natured yet oblivious member who has a dog barking or a child crying in the background; you can simply mute them until they need to speak. What may be an issue, however, are members who suddenly snap, or lose discipline, and begin causing chaos. Luckily, there are many ways to manage participants in a meeting.

If someone needs to cool off for a little bit, then you can easily move them out of the meeting and back into the Waiting Room if you have it enabled. To do this, mouse over the participant's name, click on "More" or on the "..." next to said name, then select "Put in Waiting Room." If the Waiting Room is disabled, you'll see an option that says "Put on hold" instead, which is functionally the same thing; it places the offending attendee in a timeout zone where they cannot see or hear the other participants.

A Caveat for Putting Someone in the Waiting Room/On Hold

Note that this option is also brilliant when you need to discuss sensitive information with one part of your attendees, but not the other, such as when you need to put a potential employee on hold while you discuss their interview performance with the rest of your group.

Back to dealing with disruption. In the same taskbar where you find "Put on hold," you'll also see options such as "Stop video" for offensive content, "Ask to start video" if someone needs to present, and they zoned out a bit, or "Remove" for when placing them on hold isn't enough and you need them to go. Once removed, they will not be able to rejoin by default unless you alter those settings by signing in to the Zoom web portal (https://zoom.us) and navigating to your Account Settings under Account Management. So, always opt to rather place in the Waiting Room or put on Hold first so that you have more room to amend one's judgement.

Annotation, Emotes & Chat

Annotations, emoticons and the meeting chat feature are all potent collaboration tools that help users engage with your meeting content. Annotating is enabled for the host by default, and comes into play whenever you Share Screens. You'll find you have an array of stamps, drawing tools and more, all of which are highly intuitive to use thanks to its similarities to the tools found in applications like Microsoft Word and Paint.

This lets you highlight and point out key points or items of interest on a shared screen, directing the attention of your audience. You can even add extra text if you so desire, so that people have time to take down your key points. Note that annotations on a screen are not permanent, and will disappear the moment you stop sharing; don't worry about doodling all over a document with Zoom's annotation feature, as you'll find it to still be crisp and pristine later, as if you never annotated on it at all.

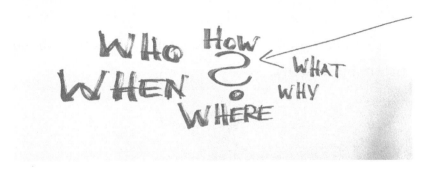

If you do not wish to share your screen per se, but still wish to use the annotation tools to get a point across, you can opt to share a blank "Whiteboard" when you click on the Share Screens feature, where you can then jot down important points as you or your participants speak. When sharing any screen that isn't the whiteboard, you can choose to manipulate its content directly by clicking on the cursor icon so that it is highlighted in blue.

To control whether participants can annotate at-will or not, sign in to your account at http://zoom.us, go into Account Management, then Account Settings, then Meeting, then Meeting (Basic). From there, you'll see the Annotation option. Check that it is enabled or not, according to your preference.

This will set the preference for all participants logging onto one of your account's meetings. You can set preferences with more precision through User Management, then Group Management, then Settings, letting you control annotation access for a specific group.

Keeping Annotation enabled will allow multiple people to annotate at once unless you change the settings to be otherwise, meaning you can jointly add notes with your peers for potent brainstorming sessions.

Emotes

Emotes, known as "reactions" in Zoom, consist of a thumbs-up sign or an icon of hands clapping. You can change the skin tone of your reactions under General Settings in your Zoom desktop app (look for the little black cog in the top right corner of your app when you log into your Zoom account). These reactions last for five seconds, and are silent, allowing a user to express a sentiment non-verbally without distracting or interrupting anyone.

Attendees can also be granted access to "non-verbal feedback," and it is highly recommended that hosts ensure this feature is enabled by, again, navigating to https://zoom.us, navigating back down to Account Settings, then Meeting, then In-Meeting (Basic) to ensure "Nonverbal Feedback" is active. By default, this feature is active, as without it users cannot Raise/Lower Hands. This feature also enables the use of symbols that stand for "faster," "slower," "yes," "no," "agree," "disagree" (thumbs up and thumbs down for those two, respectively), clapping, a teacup/coffee mug (usually meaning "I want a break"), and a clock face (usually meaning "I am not present right now").

Unlike reactions, the icons for non-verbal feedback will appear next to a participant's name until they remove it, however they can only have one non-verbal feedback icon active at a time. Contrast to reactions, where there is no limit to how many they can have at once.

Chat & File Sharing

Chat, for reasons touched on near the beginning of the book, can be a double-edged sword. It can enhance collaboration or encourage distraction, so it is best that you employ it according to the needs of your group. Once again, under your web portal's Account Settings, go to Meeting, then File Transfer. Here, you will see a bevy of options that allows you to control what kinds of files can be shared in your meeting's Chat. You can also choose to disable the File Transfer aspect of Chat entirely from here.

If left enabled, then both the host and any participant can send files by clicking on Chat in the middle of their Zoom app meeting taskbar. In the window that pops up, they'll see "File" next to the message box where they can type. Clicking on this will let them share files from either their computer, Google Drive, Dropbox, OneDrive or Box, so make sure you can trust your audience with the parameters you set.

Next, if you find that the Chat feature is being abused, yet feel that removing or putting the offenders on hold isn't viable or otherwise overkill, you can add restrictions to prevent diligent attendees from being spammed, distracted or harassed. That said, it can be better to set the restriction in advance, as then it'll feel more like a safety measure than a punishment, which will help keep the tone of your meetings positive.

To set your Chat preferences as a host, log into your Zoom app, start your meeting (a little early, if you have to), and click on Chat. In the window that pops up, click on the ellipses next to "File." Here, you'll see four tiers of chat that you can decide on for participants.

"No-One" means that Chat is effectively disabled for your meeting. No participants will be able to speak to each other or share files on Zoom, although this may feel a bit too constrictive for some.

"Host Only" means that participants can type messages and send files to you, but not to anyone else. This works comfortably if you're the sole organizer and chief presenter of this meeting. If you are sent messages or files that are relevant to the group as a whole, do not forget to Share Screens or copy/paste the message back to others.

"Everyone Publicly" is best for groups where participants are mostly motivated, but have some disruptive eggs. This allows people to freely collaborate and form ideas via files and text without interrupting the verbal part of the meeting.

"Everyone Publicly and Privately" is the default setting, but it can be problematic if people begin using your meetings as a platform to harass and cyberbully one another behind your back. If you keep this tier enabled, be especially attentive to the concerns of your attendees. This setting is not recommended if your group seems a little distracted.

Sharing Admin Powers

Managing large groups isn't always easy, nor is it desirable. When you have an important presentation to cover, or if you are chairing an important discussion, it can be jarring when you also have to constantly tend to security and community moderation. In these cases, it can help to invite a trusted individual along to the meeting solely for you to nominate them as a co-host.

To raise an attendee to the status of co-host during a meeting, you'll need to be using at least the Pro version of Zoom, although at the time of writing free accounts linked to primary and secondary schools have been known to be granted this feature too.

Before your meeting starts, make sure to go onto Zoom's web portal, log in, navigate through Account Settings, then to Meeting, then to Co-Host. Ensure the option is enabled. Then, during a meeting, bestowing co-host powers is as simple as hovering your mouse over their portrait, clicking on the ellipses next to their name, then clicking on "Make Co-Host."

This can also be done through the "Participants" or "Manage Participants" icon on the meeting control taskbar at the bottom of the window.

If Hosts are like sheriffs, then the Co-Host is like a deputy. Co-Hosts have a variety of powers like muting or disabling the video of participants, moving them into/out of the Waiting Room, sending requests for people to unmute or start their video, lock meetings, or make Zoom play a note whenever someone enters or exits, just like a Host can. A Co-Host cannot, however, exert powers such as *creating* a Waiting Room, ending the meeting for everyone, starting a meeting, or starting live-streaming.

Note that a meeting can never have more than one full Host at a time. If you are afraid you might be late for your own meeting, schedule it ahead of time so that, under Advanced Options, you can designate an Alternative Host. They will gain all the powers of a Co-Host, plus the ability to start your meeting for you should you run late.

Creating Polls

Once again, this feature requires you to at least have Zoom Pro. During Pro or higher meetings that have either been scheduled or are using Personal Meeting ID, hosts will see a "Polling" option on the meeting toolbar. As it's better to create your polls ahead of time, let's first cover how to create one for a scheduled meeting.

Once again, first ensure the feature is enabled via the Zoom web portal. You'll find the option under "Meeting."

Now that this is done, remain signed in on Zoom's website and navigate to your "Meetings" page on its web portal. Select the scheduled meeting you wish to include your poll in, or schedule a meeting from there and include your poll in that. When managing your meeting from this web page, scroll to the bottom of said page and you will see the "Poll" option. Clicking on "add" will initiate the poll creation process.

At a bare minimum, a poll needs a title, at least one question and at least one or two selectable answers for that question, depending on whether you set your poll to be single-choice or multiple-choice. From here, you can add further questions, as well as decide whether or not you want your poll to be anonymous. Note that polls, whether anonymous or not, *never* divulge who answered what to other participants, but they do give the host this information if you - as the host - choose to download the poll results after the meeting.

Hosts, as well as admins and owners of your meeting account, can download these results as CSV files via Zoom's web portal by navigating to Account Management > Reports > Usage Reports > Meeting > Report Type. From there, fill in the type and search criteria according to your needs and click Generate. You will then see your poll report, which you can now download.

Note that if you enabled anonymous polling, you will not see who answered what. Therefore, anonymous polls are great for getting a general feel of your attendees without making it personal, while at the same time they're not so great if your poll was intended as an assessment of individual knowledge or performance.

When creating an ad hoc poll in a room using your Meeting ID, the process is largely identical. Just click on your "Polling" icon in your meeting toolbar and you'll be directed to the appropriate web page in your browser.

You can also launch any existing polls from that icon when hosting scheduled meetings. Note that you can start polls whenever you choose, and while you can see the results come in at real-time, your participants cannot see what anyone else has answered unless you choose to show them after the poll closes. Once closed, a poll can be reopened; DO NOT DO THIS if you intend to keep the original results, as reopening a poll resets all data that it collected, and you won't be able to download those results later.

Excellent uses for polls, aside from personal assessments or market research among your participants, can include humorous ice-breakers to put people at ease, as well as a voting system to let your audience decide what aspect of your content will be covered today (great for more friendly environments, like a Yoga instructor asking their class what pose to cover next out of a firm selection, or an English teacher gauging which book to investigate next). They can also be used to get feedback on the meeting itself, but that is often better left to...

End-of Meeting Surveys

As you can probably guess by now, this requires navigating to "Account Management > Account Settings" after signing in to the Zoom web portal. In the Meeting tab, navigate further to the "Display end-of-meeting experience feedback survey" feature and turn it on.

From this point onwards, any time a meeting ends your participants will be able to give your meeting either a thumbs-up or a thumbs-down. This only appears at the very end of the meeting; people who are removed before the meeting is over will not be able to leave feedback. This can prevent hackers and trolls from giving misleading feedback, but can also silence valid criticism from participants if abused. Remember to handle your host powers maturely.

Those who gave a thumbs-down will then be able to specify what their issue was, although the options are mostly technical in nature (e.g. audio quality, or video displaying correctly). For feedback centered more on the content of your meeting or quality of your presentation, consider creating an anonymous poll for the end of your survey. Keeping the poll anonymous will help prevent you from taking the feedback personally along with making it easier for people to speak their minds, ergo making it easier for you to deliver a better experience next time.

Video, Recording & Background Themes

Hosting a videoconference is all well and good, but what if the information discussed is needed for future reference? What if interested participants were unable to make it due to no fault of their own, and you wish to share the content of your meetings with them? What if you wish to create a highlight reel of your meeting and upload it to social media later?

For this, you'll need to know how to record.

Presentation

If you're recording just for archival reasons, you can ignore this segment. However, if you wish to add more visual interest to yourself as the host, aside from playing around with the Video Settings in your Zoom app, you can also customize your background to set the correct tone. To do this, you'll first need to acquire a green screen; without one, your background theme cannot be laid correctly. You'll also need to ensure the room you set up in relies on strong, uniform light.

Now, your screen doesn't necessarily need to be green; it can be any strong, uniform color. But whatever color you choose, ensure you do not have clothing, hair or skin tones that match it. If you do, Zoom, won't be able to tell you apart from your background, leading to shenanigans. Once your green screen is set up, navigate back to Meeting under Account Settings on Zoom's website, then ensure "Virtual Background" is enabled.

Next, on your desktop app, go to Settings, then "Background and Filters." You can choose one of the preset backgrounds, or you can upload your own images, MP4 and MOV files. When uploading your own files, it's recommended that videos are at least 360p in quality (480x360 pixels) and that images are at least 1280 x 720 pixels. If you go smaller, make sure the image matches your camera's aspect ratio.

Finally, sign out of your desktop app, then sign back in again, and you should find your virtual background has taken effect.

Recording as Host & Co-Host

There are two kinds of recording; local, and cloud-based. All forms of Zoom account can record locally provided it's via a desktop app, while all devices with Zoom can record via cloud as long as you're using Zoom Pro and above.

To record locally as the host, simply hit the Record button on your meeting taskbar once the meeting commences. You'll see the icon change into options to pause or stop the recording, and you'll see a little recording bar in the top left of your meeting window. You can start, pause and stop this recording whenever you like. In

Zoom, the difference between stopping and pausing is that stopping means you'll generate another video file when you begin recording again, while pausing means you'll just keep adding to your current video file instead.

When the meeting ends all video files, along with audio-only versions, will be saved to your machine as MP4 and M4A files respectively, and you can specify where they are saved too. You can even upload these files to a cloud-based service like Google Drive later if you wish, meaning it's possible for free Zoom accounts to still have file sharing with their recordings, even if it's in a bit of a roundabout way.

Note that if your meeting's Chat was used while you were recording, said chat will be saved as a TXT file as well, and you can further tweak your local recording preferences to your liking in your desktop app's Settings, under the Recording tab.

To perform a cloud-based recording as a host, make sure the feature is enabled under Account Settings on Zoom's website in the Recording tab, then - if you need to - tweak the rest of the settings according to your needs.

When you are in a Zoom meeting, hover your mouse over the Record button on the meeting taskbar. You should now see a little "^" arrow next to it. Click on that arrow, then select "Record to cloud." It is as simple as that. When the meeting is over, all cloud recordings will be processed by Zoom, who'll send an email to your host email address when the processing has finished. You'll also be given two links in said email; an admin link to let you manage your account's recordings as a whole, and a participant link that others can watch without constituting an innate security risk.

Recording as Participant

If you want participants to be able to create local recordings just like you, simply click on Participants/Manage Participants during a meeting, click on either "More" or the ellipses next to the participant's name, then select "Allow Record." This affords recording privileges to that one individual. You can assign and take away these privileges from as many of your participants as you wish at will, but you will have to do so manually for each one.

Participants can never perform direct cloud-based recordings.

Zoom & Calendly

As both Calendly and Zoom work well with Google Calendar, you may have asked yourself, "Can Calendly and Zoom work well together too?"

After all, Calendly is a highly useful app that streamlines the decision-making process when trying to figure out the date for a meeting. It eliminates all the time-consuming back-and-forth one tends to experience when trying to set meeting dates through emails or phone calls.

To use Calendly, go to https://calendly.com/and click on "Sign Up." You'll be walked through the process by Calendly without complications. From there, you can create your own events (such as meeting schedules) through an intuitive and tooltip-laden UI. Once you've set the days available for your meeting and generated your event, you can share its link with others, who can give their feedback on which time and date would work best for them, as well as times that aren't ideal for them, but could still work. You can then use this data to choose a time that the majority finds acceptable. In any case, the process is short, sweet and simple.

Normally, however, you'd still need to create and schedule your meeting manually in Zoom. This is fine, especially if you're on a tight budget, as just by using Calendly on its own to determine an ideal meeting time you have already saved yourself a heap of time and prevented much dithering.

If you wish to combine Zoom and Calendly more intimately however, go to https://calendly.com/integrations, then click on "Zoom." Make sure all the requirements are fulfilled (usually, this involves having a Premium Calendly account), then click on "Connect Zoom." If you are not an admin or sole owner for your Zoom account, get in touch with one, so they can pre-approve Calendly for your Zoom app here: https://marketplace.zoom.us/apps/BF4eht18S3a0KTLiKM3P0A.

Once Zoom and Calendly are linked for you, then in Calendly you'll find that the next time you create or edit an Event, you can add a location for it. Just beneath the "Add a Location" bar, you'll see "Zoom" in bright blue letters. Click here, and just like that your Calendly Event will automatically schedule a corresponding Zoom meeting once you've finalized the date and time. It also means that the conference details of your meeting will automatically be provided to the participants who helped book/finalize a time.

Once again, a short process, sweet and simple.

If you aren't a fan of Calendly, Zapier.com and Zoom.ai can both potentially fill your schedule-automation needs.

I hate
monday

OPEN

Tue - Fri   8.00 AM - 6.00 PM

Sat - Sun 10.00 AM - 6.00 PM

Slow Hands

Recurring Meetings

Whenever you are scheduling a meeting with an automatically generated ID in your Zoom desktop client or mobile app, you have the option of making that meeting Recurring or Repeating. This feature works well when you need to host a similar topic with a set crowd at regular intervals, like a yoga teacher giving classes, or a spiritual leader providing a virtual space for their congregation.

When a meeting is set as Recurring, then all the settings you specify for it will remain unchanged, including link, passcode and Meeting ID. For this reason, it is recommended that you never use your Personal Meeting ID for Recurring meetings, as the value and utility of your PMID is that it is constant even for Instant meetings, and this value gets lost if you reserve it according to a strict recurring schedule when an automatically generated ID would've fulfilled the same role in this case.

Anyway, once the rest of your meeting settings are finalized, select the calendar you wish to add to (or just select "Add to Calendar" if applicable), then select "Schedule." It is highly recommended that you schedule using Google Calendar.

When doing so, you'll then be prompted by Google to sign in and select your Google Account if you haven't already, and may be asked to let Zoom access your Google account. Allow Zoom to do so. You will then be shown options for how your meeting should recur; daily, weekly on the day you set (e.g. every Wednesday if your meeting will first commence on a Wednesday), monthly, annually, every weekday, or some other custom arrangement.

When you're happy with the way your scheduled meeting will recur, select "Save."

You can also use Outlook as your calendar if your Zoom app is on a mobile device, where the process is highly similar. You can technically use Outlook on Windows and Mac too, but it is not recommended; Google Calendar is far simpler and easier to use in this case, especially if you're also using Calendly.

Joining Multiple Meetings at Once

This feature is restricted to those with the Business tier of Zoom or higher, although Pro and free users likely won't have much call for it anyway. To ensure everyone linked to your account can join multiple meetings at once, sign into the Zoom web portal, then navigate back down to "Account Settings," then "Meeting," then "In Meeting (Basic)." Finally, enable "Join different meetings simultaneously on desktop." As you can likely guess, this feature isn't possible for mobile devices.

If you do not want everyone attached to your account using this power, then in the web portal you should instead navigate to "User Management" then "Group Management." If you haven't done so already, use "Add Group" to fill a list with contacts who you wish to use as support staff, or whatever other roles you feel will need to view multiple meetings at once. When your desired group exists under your account, stay under "Group Management" and select said group. Then go "Settings," then "Meeting," then continue the process similarly to how it was described in the last paragraph.

Setting up Live Streams & Webinars

This process isn't too different from setting up a conference like in Chapter 2, but there are some nuances to be aware of.

Webinars

An option for holding absolutely massive virtual public events, webinars allow between 100-10,000 view-only participants. This means they can use the chat feature to ask questions if enabled, but cannot speak directly and aren't as likely to interact with one another. Depending on chat settings, they may not interact with one another at all. You can have a further 100 panelists on top of this - participants who can speak and use their cameras. Webinars are only available to those with a Pro account or higher who have also purchased the Webinar add-on, and can only be used by users who have been licensed. You can purchase the add-on by signing in to your account's Billing page here https://zoom.us/signin#webinar.

You can then, as the account Owner or Admin, assign the add-on to one of your Account users by signing in to Zoom's website, then going to "User Management," then to "Users." Click "Edit" at the end of the Username that you wish to assign the license to, then ensure that "Licensed," then "Webinar" is ticked. Then, click "Save."

To set up a webinar, stay logged into the Zoom website, then go to "Webinars," then "Schedule a Webinar." You'll see the process is much like scheduling a meeting, and you'll even see the option to make your webinars recurring. By this point, you should be able to choose the options you want on or off without hand-holding.

Note that if you require participants to register, you can have them answer a pre-meeting questionnaire. You can do this via the Zoom web portal by going Webinars > Invitations > Approval > Edit, then navigating to the "Questions" and "Custom Questions" tabs. Do not forget to save when you're done. You can add your panelists while under "Invitations" too, by clicking on its own "Edit" button. Non-panelists are invited simply through the "Copy the invitation" and "Email me the invitation" options next to your webinar's name.

Once your webinar is set up, you can start it via Zoom's website, or via your Zoom app through logging in, going under "Meetings," then finding your webinar and clicking "Start."

Aside from the addition of panelists and the potentially huge attendee sizes, Webinars have many of the features present in normal Zoom meetings. Consider using Mute All, Co-Hosts and participant size add-ons as alternatives if you aren't sure a Webinar is what you need for your strategy. Note that there are no Reactions, Waiting Room or File Transfer features in a Zoom webinar.

Live Streams

Live-streaming is a feature that lets your Zoom meeting broadcast in real time to other media platforms, allowing you to reach audiences on YouTube, Facebook and more. Live streams can be enabled for both regular meetings and webinars, but again require an account of Pro or higher. To ensure live-streaming has been enabled for you, as an admin you can log onto Zoom's website and go Account Management > Account Settings > In Meeting (Advanced) > "Allow live-streaming the meetings."

Then, check the streaming services you wish to be able to use. For webinars, this can be done via Account Management > Webinar Settings > Edit. If you wish to use a custom streaming service, be sure to check that option, then provide a Stream URL, a Page URL and a Stream Key where you're prompted for instructions, so hosts will be able to use that custom option should they wish.

Then, when you wish to host a live-streaming meeting, log into Zoom's website. Click on "Meetings." Then, schedule a new meeting. When you click "Save," investigate the Advanced Options that pop up. You'll see which platforms your meeting will be able to stream to, as well as instructions for how to commence live-streaming in your Zoom app. If you wish to use a custom service, click on "configure live stream settings" now. This will let you fill in the Stream URL, Page URL and Stream Key for your custom service now, so you won't need to worry about doing so when trying to livestream mid-meeting.

Chapter 4: The Future of Video Conferencing

Why Video Conferencing Is Better Than Phonecalls/ Emails

(a.k.a the reason why not everyone who reads the Gettysburg Address sounds like Abraham Lincoln)

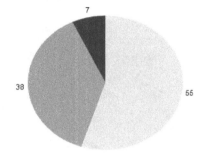

- Percentage Impact of Words in Communicating Intention, Assuming a Common Language
- Percentage Impact of Tone of Voice in Communicating Intention, Assuming a Common Language
- Percentage Impact of Facial Expression in Communicating Intention, Assuming a Common Language

Risk Management vs Forward-Thinking

Switching to new technology, or new methods of working, can be daunting. However, while change carries an active risk, it is also true that stagnation carries a risk of its own. The choice then is whether you want your risk to be active or passive; whether you want to choose your risk, or whether you want your risk to choose you.

While reading this book, you may have noted that while it has been helpful, it isn't quite the same as having someone explain it to you face-to-face with passion or kindness. For this reason, you'll never know me if I walk down the street, nor do you

66

necessarily feel any special kinship toward me - it'd take many, many more books for that.

Compare and contrast to meeting face-to-face. You might decide within fifteen seconds that you like someone, or will get along with them. Or, if not, you're more likely to notice what may be off about them, which in turn gives you the opportunity to build a strong rapport through empathy. All this is made possible through visual communication and body language. Videoconferencing is what allows you to retain this powerful force multiplier across vast distances.

Always bear this in mind when deciding whether it is worth investing more in your videoconferencing service or not. Bear this in mind when deciding whether to stick with an app you know, or accepting a few minor hassles to switch over to one that allows you to connect much more reliably to the colleagues and customers you depend on as a businessman or businesswoman.

If your business relies a lot on travelling for meeting purposes, I strongly recommend you upgrade to at least a basic version of Zoom. Not only does it save you fuel and accommodation costs, it can earn you brownie points with environmentalists for some neat PR as you can (truthfully) claim you use videoconferencing to reduce the waste that so often plagues the excessive catering, disposable cups, crumpled papers and other derelict leftovers generated by traditional meetings.

In a world where we grapple with inflation and potential resource scarcity, videoconferencing could buy the time needed to reach the next innovative idea, and will save you plenty of money regardless. Even Zoom's most expensive plan, at $19.99 per host, per month, is often cheaper than the average $100 cost per person per night for a hotel stay in the U.S.A. (Lock, 2020).

Hardware & Tech

The more you rely on videoconferencing, however, the more you should consider investing in better audio-visual equipment. A bad microphone can make you sound soft, or drown the meeting in a low humming drone. A mediocre microphone might add a little fuzziness to your voice, or cut out from time to time, necessitating repetition and ruining your annunciation, all of which make it harder for you to be understood.

Meanwhile, operating without a webcam can negate the entire point of using videoconferencing; without video, you may as well take a phone-call or write an email for all the good it does. A poor webcam, meanwhile, can cause much of the subtlety in your expressions to be lost, and no one likes looking at an overly-blurry or pixelated image.

If you find yourself experiencing these issues no matter how you tweak your audio or video settings, strongly consider upgrading so that your face can appear bright and vivid, your voice crisp and clear. This is especially important if you're the host, or if you are especially important to the meeting in some other way (e.g. if a group of management staff are interviewing you to see if you can meet a job's requirements, you are where all the attention will be, so you'll want to make sure your tech isn't holding back your neatness and presentation). You especially don't want to sound muffled, robotic and squeaky when you speak, so certainly invest in an external microphone for a more organic, deep and rich-sounding video-conferencing voice.

External microphones and webcams are always recommended over integrated ones due to nearly always being of significantly better quality. For a reliable hardware provider, try Logitech for microphones, webcams and even headsets.

Location, Location, Location

Aside from purchasing additional hardware, you can also improve the professionalism of your presentation through a few simple tricks.

For your webcam, the general rule is to set it just above your eye-level, facing you at a subtle downwards angle. Setting it lower than this might make you look arrogant, uncanny or boorish, while setting it higher than this will make you seem puny. When set just right, you will look approachable, but not ignorable. Pay attention to the angle from which entertainers and film stars are viewed during their most dynamic and glamorous close-ups.

For optimal lighting that accentuates the life in your face, consider placing a working daylight bulb around 4 feet away from your webcam to the left and right on either side. Clamp lights are best for this, but floor or table lamps will do in a pinch.

Next, to improve the acoustics in your room with little-to-no budget, drape thick curtains over all windows in your room to decrease reverberation caused by the glass. Placing your props or furniture to occupy the corners of your room will also prevent deeper sounds from building up too strongly. Next, make sure all doors and windows are closed during your meetings, as this will prevent external noises from making unwanted impacts.

To ensure that wind (or even your own breathing) does not disrupt or distort your speech, it's also highly recommended that you invest in a microphone wind-shield or pop-filter, even if it's just a cheap or basic one, as the difference compared to not using one at all can be huge. Finally, to guarantee your voice is captured perfectly from this point on, always be sure to speak directly into your microphone as placing it even a few inches too far can cause your voice to become unbearably soft.

Conclusion

By this point, you have now learned everything needed to start using Zoom with confidence. Although further reading is recommended for managers in larger businesses, those at free or Pro level will find that what they have learned will let them navigate through Zoom's bevy of features with poise and ease. Once you get the hang of Zoom, you'll also be in a better mental space to use other similar software too; even if the layout and features aren't all the same, you'll find you've gained a more intuitive understanding of what quality video-conferencing software can do, what to expect from it, and roughly where to find what you need from it.

This will stand you in good stead as more and more businesses and individuals alike turn to videoconferencing to fulfill their needs, as you'll have an easier time engaging with an ever-growing audience or market. Anywhere where people have and value the internet, there will be an opportunity to reach out to people through videoconferences. In a world where fuel becomes more and more precious, this will only become more and more true.

It is recommended that you keep this book handy as you go for the time being, spending the next few months always turning back to it to revise its advice, although as you grow more and more advanced, and as Zoom gains more and more updates, you'll increasingly find a potent companion in the company's own website, where you can learn all about its latest features and how to work with specific devices.

However, no matter what changes, Zoom will likely remain a socially sensitive and user-friendly application, reinforcing Eric Yuan's dream of helping young lovers look into each others' eyes without having to wait a whole month or endure a grueling 10-hour train ride.

This is likely why even the free version allows you to hold a conversation for eternity when it's kept small and intimate. For those who do not need to hold massive meetings with their division or department, but just want to see the faces of their family again, Zoom still has them covered.

And yet, for those whose interests are professionally inclined, Zoom carries nearly every feature you could want in delivering a compelling talk to scores of people at a time, each one of whom could be connecting from anywhere in the world.

This could be you, doing all these things, right now. Potentially for free. Whatever you decide to do from this point, I hope Zoom helps make the process easier for you, whether you're trying to land your next interview, host a long-awaited reunion or set up your own small business to stay afloat and realize your dreams.

References

Aksa2011. (2016). Camera Webcam Computer Internet Black Electronics. In *Pixabay*. https://pixabay.com/photos/camera-webcam-computer-internet-1219748/

Altmann, G. (2018). Business Office Training Problem Solution. In *Pixabay*. https://pixabay.com/photos/business-office-training-problem-3694993/

Ameen, M. (2015). Web Cam Internet Video Communication Web Chat. In *Pixabay*. https://pixabay.com/photos/web-cam-internet-video-796227/

antonbe. (2020). Zoom Webcam Video Communication Chat Internet Web. In *Pixabay*. https://pixabay.com/photos/zoom-webcam-video-communication-5064083/

Cameron, J. (2020). Photo of Boy Sitting on Chair While Holding an Ipad. In *Pexels*. https://www.pexels.com/photo/photo-of-boy-sitting-on-chair-while-holding-an-ipad-4144095/

CoxinhaFotos. (2017). Destruction Cube 3d Matter Solid Disruption. In *Pixabay*. https://pixabay.com/illustrations/destruction-cube-3d-matter-solid-2584744/

de Richelieu, A. (2020). Child Taking Classes Online. In *Pexels*. https://www.pexels.com/photo/child-taking-classes-online-4261786/

Ellis, M. (2019, June 13). *How to Use Calendly - Calendly*. Zapier. https://zapier.com/apps/calendly/tutorials/how-to-use-calendly

Hassan, M. (2018). Hat Cowboy Stetson Western Rodeo Head Fashion. In *Pixabay*. https://pixabay.com/vectors/hat-cowboy-stetson-western-rodeo-3722602/

Hutt, M. (2017, August 9). *The Future of Video Conferencing*. ezTalks. https://www.eztalks.com/video-conference/future-of-video-conferencing.html

Johnson, D. (2020, June 24). *What Is Zoom and How Does It Work?* Lifewire. https://www.lifewire.com/what-is-zoom-and-how-does-it-work-4800476

Lakshmohan. (2020, May 24). *Discord Vs Zoom: An In-Depth Comparison*. My URL Pro. https://myurlpro.com/discord-vs-zoom-an-in-depth-comparison/

Lock, S. (2020, July 23). *Hotels: Average Daily Rate US 2020*. Statista. https://www.statista.com/statistics/208133/us-hotel-revenue-per-available-room-by-month/

Natesan, P., & du Plessis, P. (2020, August 12). *Company boards must be innovative to stay ahead of the curve*. IOL. https://www.iol.co.za/business-report/opinion/company-boards-must-be-innovative-to-stay-ahead-of-the-curve-096777ab-a456-487a-a2ce-157cb3e2ca95

Negative Space. (2016). Grayscale Photo of Computer Laptop Near White Notebook and Ceramic Mug on Table. In *Pexels*. https://www.pexels.com/photo/grayscale-photo-of-computer-laptop-near-white-notebook-and-ceramic-mug-on-table-169573/

OpenClipart-Vectors. (2013). Sheriff Badge Cowboy Deputy Lawman Marshal Outlaw. In *Pixabay*.

https://pixabay.com/vectors/sheriff-badge-cowboy-deputy-lawman-156649/

Pexels. (2016). Audio Close-Up Electricity Electronics Equipment. In *Pixabay*. https://pixabay.com/photos/audio-close-up-electricity-1867121/

Piatanova, T. (2020). *Zoom for Students – Zoom Tutorials*. Pacific University Wordpress Community. http://web5.lib.pacificu.edu/zoom/students/

Pixabay. (2016). Conference Room. In *Pexels*. https://www.pexels.com/photo/chairs-conference-room-corporate-indoors-236730/

Pixabay. (2017). Train Track. In *Pexels*. https://www.pexels.com/photo/country-countryside-daylight-field-533630/

Shvets, A. (2020a). People on a Video Call. In *Pexels*. https://www.pexels.com/photo/people-on-a-video-call-4226140/

Shvets, A. (2020b). People on a Video Call. In *Pexels*. https://www.pexels.com/photo/people-on-a-video-call-4226263/

Smith, D. (2019, August 29). *The Importance of Face-to-Face Communication in the Modern Workforce*. Lifesize. https://www.lifesize.com/en/video-conferencing-blog/importance-face-to-face-communication

Subiyanto, K. (2020). Glad black female worker with signboard at entrance of cafeteria. In *Pexels*. https://www.pexels.com/photo/glad-black-female-worker-with-signboard-at-entrance-of-cafeteria-4349752/

Unuth, N. (2020, March 13). *Here's Why You Should Start Video Conferences*. Lifewire. https://www.lifewire.com/benefits-of-video-conferencing-4108480

Wheeler, J. (2018). Passing Train on the Tracks. In *Pexels*. https://www.pexels.com/photo/passing-train-on-the-tracks-1598075/

Zoom. (2020). *Frequently asked questions for admins*. Zoom Help Center. https://support.zoom.us/hc/en-us/articles/360042443452-Frequently-asked-questions-for-admins

Zoom Video Communications. (2020). *Zoom Video Communications Mission, Vision & Values*. Comparably.

https://www.comparably.com/companies/zoom-video-communications/mission

CPSIA information can be obtained
at www.ICGtesting.com
Printed in the USA
LVHW021108160221
679322LV00015B/722

9 781914 284489